PRINT CASEBOOKS 2/SECOND ANNUAL EDITION
THE BEST IN ENVIRONMENTAL GRAPHICS

PRINT CASEBOOKS 2
SECOND ANNUAL EDITION
THE BEST IN ENVIRONMENTAL GRAPHICS

Conceived by
Martin Fox

Text and Introduction by
Stanley Abercrombie

Published by
RC Publications, Inc.
Washington, D.C.

Published by RC Publications, Inc.
6400 Goldsboro Road NW
Washington, D.C. 20034

Manufactured in U.S.A.
First Printing 1977

**PRINT CASEBOOKS 2/SECOND
ANNUAL EDITION/THE BEST IN
ENVIRONMENTAL GRAPHICS**
Library of Congress Catalog Card
Number 75-123-94
ISBN 0-915734-13-3

**PRINT CASEBOOKS 2/SECOND
ANNUAL EDITION**
Complete 6-Volume Set
ISBN 0-915734-10-9

RC PUBLICATIONS
President and Publisher: Robert Cadel
Vice President and Editor: Martin Fox
Art Director/Designer: Andrew P. Kner
Assistant Editor: Ellen-Jane Opat
Associate Art Director: Rose M. DeNeve
Business Manager: Howard Cadel
Title Page Illustration: Isadore Seltzer

Whenever something happens for the second time, we inevitably make comparisons. This is the second annual edition of the Environmental Graphics Casebook, and, while two occurrences hardly enable us to make long-range predictions, it is true that this new collection is noticeably different from the previous one, and that these differences reflect changes in the profession.

Most obvious, perhaps, is the change in building types for which environmental graphics programs have been designed. Whereas the first Casebook included six graphics programs for large commercial centers, three systems of transportation symbols, and two commissions for resort communities, the present collection is quite different; there is not even one program for a large commercial center. There are, instead, one nationwide and one province-wide signing program, two restaurants, two airports, and—building types not represented at all last year—two hospitals and two zoos. (Well, there *was* an aquarium last year, but that's not exactly the same.) Hospitals, in fact, seem at the moment to be a predominant source of environmental graphics commissions: fully a quarter of submissions to this year's Casebook were hospital jobs.

What this indicates, of course, is that the client has changed for the designer working in environmental graphics; he isn't being asked to do as many large commercial complexes these

days simply because fewer of them are being planned and built. Indeed, approximately two-thirds of this Casebook's selections are not for private commercial ventures at all, but for educational, institutional, public or semi-public clients. That shows pretty clearly where the money was in 1976, or, at least, where it was being spent.

Another characteristic of the present selections is that roughly a third of them deal with problems of either bilingual or completely non-lingual communication, using murals or pictographs (not just pictures, but pictures imparting information) to supplement or even substitute for writing. In addition, one of the projects (Pontiac Stadium) is concerned with communication to those whose sight is color-impaired, while another (Knoxville Zoo) has planned the addition of Braille for those without sight.

But *environmental* graphics differ most markedly from just plain *graphics* in that they are designed not just to transmit messages, but also to reinforce—even, at times, to create—environmental character. Many examples included here (the Montreal Airport restaurants, the Harvard library mural, or Our Lady of Lourdes Hospital) even perform the second function without the first: they don't say a word, and they don't need to.

An expression of admiration for non-verbal design, by the way, shouldn't be confused with admiration for what we might call anti-verbal design. Two of the selected projects,

while visually handsome, have at their heart a disrespect for language. In environmental graphics, just as in more traditional graphics, the basis of good design is clear communication, and the basis of clear communication—to a literate audience—is correct language. The use of jargon and the invention of new "words" are reprehensible, however stylish their appearance.

Increasing dependence on non-verbal communication parallels a growing maturity of the environmental graphics field and a growing confidence of its members in their separate identity. A milestone in establishing such identity was an initial discussion, in 1973, among several environmental graphics designers about the need for forming their own professional organization. Their concern was on two levels: first, the need to counteract some negative experiences among past clients of such work, and, second but related, the need for making the profession more readily understood. The needed understanding, they felt, was being diluted by some who were then calling themselves environmental graphics designers but who, rather than dealing seriously with the sensory perceptions of surfaces and spaces, were really only selling a product.

This concerned little group, now called the Society of Environmental Graphics Designers, has grown considerably, and in 1976, was officially registered in California as a non-profit professional society. A recent project undertaken by the SEGD shows very well how much there is for such an organization to do.

The federal government's General Services Administration, a frequent client for all sorts of graphics work, asked the SEGD to help determine a reasonable fee scale for environmental graphics jobs. What the SEGD team found, upon investigation, was that designers' fee proposals for a single GSA job ranged all the way from $9000 to $75,000. Clearly, the $75,000 job would have been more inclusive than the cheaper version, but, clearly also, the profession had been operating without generally accepted answers to some very basic questions: What is the range of its services? What is the range of its fees for those services? And how should a prospective client evaluate proposals for such services and fees?

Progress is being made toward standardizing answers to these questions. The SEGD has furnished the GSA with guidelines for evaluating proposals from both graphics designers and fabricators, and looks forward to more work with the GSA.

A remarkable feature of this year's Casebook is that five of the selections are Canadian. Even more remarkable is that three of these five are the designs of a single firm, Jacques Guillon/Designers Inc. of Montreal. And perhaps most remarkable of all is that the three Guillon projects are so varied; Guillon's approach is obviously not a single

dogmatic style, but rather a dogged attention to particular requirements. *Salut, monsieur.*

Yet another characteristic of these selections—a detail, and yet one which cannot escape our notice—is the prevalence of Helvetica typeface. In his introduction to the first Environmental Graphics Casebook, Edward K. Carpenter wrote that one thing the majority of projects had in common was the "typeface selected...Helvetica." Indeed, fully two-thirds of the selected projects used Helvetica. Yet the present collection of projects represents an even greater proportion— approximately three-fourths have used Helvetica in some part of their design. In addition, a couple of other selected projects have used Swiss Helvetica's slightly younger, and closely related, French cousin, Univers.

A few observers have reacted with alarm to the growing popularity of these "New Grotesque" faces. A recent article by Leslie Savan appeared in New York's weekly *Village Voice*; its headline (in—what else?—Helvetica) proclaimed that "This Typeface Is Changing Your Life." What followed was an almost hysterical warning against Helvetica brainwashing, in which James Wines, co-director of SITE (Sculpture in the Environment) was quoted as saying that "Helvetica is part of a psychological enslavement." Few of us consider it quite that sinister.

Rather, Helvetica seems to be, at worst, a bit boring. At

best, we seem to be finding in this more than two decade-old face a standard for our time—clean, bland, comfortably familiar, and, as that familiarity increases, quickly and easily read. That doesn't seem a bad thing to have around.

The projects presented in this Casebook were chosen, after a long day's deliberation and after the viewing of well over a thousand slides, by a jury of five: Susan Braybrooke, Merle Westlake, Al Corchia, Ken Resen, and Lance Wyman. The work of the judges' own firms, as will be seen, was not prohibited from competition. Authorship of all work, however, was anonymous during the judging, and judges kept modestly silent when their own firms' work was shown.

Observing the jury in action, one had to be impressed with its repeated agreement. There were, certainly, a number of debated projects (some of them were finally included, some were not), but, for the most part, hands went up (or stayed down) with surprising unanimity. What such unanimity suggests is something very heartening: that, despite the recent emergence of environmental graphics as a separate field, and despite the great variety of both problems and solutions within that field, there are in operation well established and widely respected criteria for environmental graphics evaluation.

Such criteria, no matter how strongly felt, are partly

intuitive and are notoriously difficult to put into words. These, perhaps, come close: visual appeal, functional legibility, and the sense of appropriate character. But perhaps such verbalization isn't even necessary. For this Casebook at least, the highest standards of the environmental graphics profession are implicit in the 25 selected projects.
—*Stanley Abercrombie*

CASEBOOK JURORS

Al Corchia

Kenneth Resen

Susan Braybrooke

Lance Wyman

Wyman is a principal in the firm of Wyman & Cannan, design consultants whose services range from corporate identity programs to architectural graphics systems and exhibit design. Former work experience was with General Motors, George Nelson and Lance Wyman/Peter Murdoch Partnership. His work has been published in numerous magazines, trade publications and books, among them: Esquire, Fortune, Architectural Forum, PRINT and Graphis Annual. In addition, Wyman's designs have been exhibited at the Museum of Modern Art, the Louvre and the Smithsonian.

Except for a four-year interlude when he joined Rudolph de Harak to form Corchia, de Harak, Inc., Al Corchia has been head of his own design firm, first The Corchia Group, Inc., and now, Al Corchia, Inc. He has designed for some of the largest corporations and foundations in the country, as well as for government agencies. Among his many clients are: AT&T, Corning Glass Works, Georg Jensen, the U.S. Department of Interior and the Wall Street Journal. Corchia is a member of AIGA, and is president of the National Association of Design and Art Service Organizations.

Since 1966, Resen has been a partner in the design firm of Page, Arbitrio & Resen, Ltd. His previous design experience was with I.M. Pei and Associates Graphics Department and Page Graphics. His work has been published in such periodicals as Progressive Architecture, PRINT and Industrial Design and he has received awards from the AIGA, Type Directors Club, Mead Paper Company and Financial World. Resen is a member of AIGA and serves on the Architectural Board of Reviews of the Village of Mamaroneck, NY.

Currently the acquisitions editor for the Whitney Library of Design, Braybrooke has had considerable experience as an architectural editor and writer. Her credits include: assistant editor of Architectural Record, associate editor of House Beautiful's Special Publications and director of publications and associate of the firm Caudill Rowlett Scott. As a specialist in the field of communications, she has acted as information officer for a welfare organization for the elderly, and helped set up a new central enrollment system for the British universities.

Merle T. Westlake

Westlake is vice president and director of Hugh Stubbins and Associates, Inc., in Cambridge, MA. He has designed and executed limited editions of serigraphs as well as large environmental graphics for office buildings in Cambridge, at MIT and other educational institutions, and he produced environmental graphics and designed books for Harvard. Westlake is a member of the Boston Society of Architects, the American Institute of Architects and AIGA.

CASEBOOK WRITER

Stanley Abercrombie

Abercrombie is a registered architect in New York who has won awards for both design and journalism. He was a recent Loeb Fellow for Advanced Environmental Studies at Harvard's Graduate School of Design, and in 1974 he was the U.S. representative on the awards jury of the *Union Internationale d'Architecture* in Paris. He is a former senior editor of Architecture Plus and is presently editor of Interiors.

Pusey Library Mural

Environmental graphics need not always be identifying signs. They can also serve as emblems of the character of a building. The Pusey library mural, ''Renaissance Constructed Capitals,'' is a handsome example.

Although this Casebook is intended to recognize graphic *systems*, not just single units, the judges felt that, because the mural was so large (over a hundred feet long and a wall high), and because it contributed so much to its whole environment, the spirit—if not the letter—of the competition rules was well fulfilled.

The mural is an important feature in a public corridor of Harvard University's new library named for former president Nathan Marsh Pusey. The library was designed by Hugh Stubbins and Associates as an underground structure, thus interrupting as little as possible the school's famous Yard.

Conceived by Stubbins' own graphics department, the mural is partly hand-painted, partly silk-screened. Evocative of the tradition of literature and history which the library represents, the central section of the wall is based on the calculations of five different Renaissance calligraphers for the geometric construction of ideally proportioned capital letters.

These constructions, as well as the adjacent wall areas, are crisply presented in brown-black lines, with occasional vermilion accents, on an ivory ground. The capitals thus constructed,

Photos: Dave Bailey

3.

however, are not painted in; they are therefore not immediately perceived. The mural, then, becomes a persistently intriguing visual game—what *are* those lines and circle indicating? What they're indicating, of course, are capital letters spelling out the name PUSEY, or rather, in the strict Roman letter tradition, PVSEY.

Client: The President and Fellows of Harvard College
Design firm: Hugh Stubbins and Associates, Cambridge, MA
Designer: Merle Westlake
Fabricator: John Wilson Doherty—Foster Sign Co.
Other consultants: William Bond—Houghton Library, Harvard University; Sherwin Williams Paint Co.

4.

1, 2. Letter construction details.
3. The details combined as a mural.
4. In place at the Harvard library.

When the industry began, a telephone was a telephone. Now, with the burgeoning of different shapes, services, colors, and billing arrangements, there are telephones and then there are telephones. With this welcome variety has also come some quite unwelcome bewilderment on the part of telephone customers trying to make a choice, and even some outright aggravation for those trying to schedule an appointment with a "Ma Bell" representative.

"Telephones & Telephones" is a prototype for a chain of shops intended to change all that. Its design—indeed, the whole marketing concept—is the work of the industrial design firm of Robert P. Gersin Associates, Inc., with Louis Nelson as program director. Serving just one neighborhood from a shopping center in Colonie, New York, at first, the design had to be flexible enough to be adapted to hundreds of other locations and in spaces of varied shape ranging from 1500 square feet in area to over 3000 square feet.

The triangular display units are each composed of three panels, with possibilities for interchanging panels, for substituting new panels for outmoded old ones, and for moving whole units about to fit a particular layout. A ceiling grid integrated with the design allows lighting to follow the triangular units wherever they go. Each panel is designed to give information about one aspect of telephone service—for

example, "Styles and Colors," "Special Needs," or "Get More and Save." Brochures are available at many panels, but basically the information is given by—what else?—telephone. Customers are encouraged to browse freely from panel to panel, picking up telephones and listening to recorded messages when they want to know more. If some questions are still unanswered, a company representative is available, but generally the customer feels unencumbered by salesmanship, and company man-hours are minimized, too.

The graphics program includes much more than the interior displays. Counters for service personnel and cashiers, informal customer seating areas, brochures, shopping bags, a special entrance and window design, and guidelines for general exterior appearance—all were also part of Gersin Associates' work.

Inside, display panels have silk-screened lettering on birch plywood, with lacquered finishes. Wall graphics— including a gigantic "Hello"—are executed in vinyl. Outside, materials are Plexiglas, glass, and aluminum. Although the ubiquitous Helvetica Medium typeface is used for large areas of text, the headlines and most prominent signs use Plantin Bold for a distinctive "signature." Colors are generally warm and bright—pale tans with strong hues of red, yellow, brown, blue, and magenta.

Such a facility, with all its

1.

2.

3.

1, 2. On the entrance wall, multiple
repetitions of the Plantin Bold
"signature" double as safety
markings on the glass.
3. Interior is brightened by a reflective
metal ceiling. Customers can pick up
telephones for recorded
information.

implications for a giant corporation's whole marketing approach is, naturally, not a quick job. The idea and its physical expression have been developing over a number of years, with many demonstrations (in both model form and full-scale mock-ups) to test the results. Nor is this prototype necessarily the final version: after its first six months of operation, a series of post-design studies were undertaken by the client to determine what adjustments or changes—if any—had to be made and incorporated into the design of further installations.

4.

5.

Client: American Telephone & Telegraph, New York Telephone
Design firm: Robert P. Gersin Associates, Inc., New York
Designers: Louis Nelson, Program Director; Ingrid Caruso, Lee Stout, Interior Designers; Paul Hanson, Graphic Design
Fabricator: CD Industries
Other consultants: James DeStephano (electrical); Michael Mastrangelo (audio-visual)

4, 5. *Triangular display units are easily moved to vary the layouts.*

Mirabel Airport Restaurants

Some entries in this year's Casebook competition caused the judges to yawn a bit; a few others produced a groan. But the only entry to cause them to laugh out loud was this one from Jacques Guillon/Designers Inc., of Montreal. It also made them think of breaking for lunch, for this program is both lighthearted and appetizing.

The design solution is actually double-pronged— composed of graphics for two separate restaurants within the new Mirabel Airport at Montreal. The Guillon firm has also designed a complete signing program for the airport itself, which is also a Casebook winner and can be found on page 18.

For the two restaurant programs, each comprising the design and production of large wall graphics, area identification signs, and menus, Guillon was given a year's time and a total budget of $13,700. The firm assigned three designers to the dual project.

Above a built-in banquette in one of the restaurants, Le Café Campagne, a wall area 6′ high and 20′ long was given a photographic blowup of onions and apples. Lettering is in apple red and in Pluto typeface with a distinctly well-fed look.

The other restaurant, L'Eclair, features a 22′ long painting of just that pastry, in various stages of disappearing down a very Grand Opera throat, and with the supporting cast of fox fur stole trying to get some of the action.

Both L'Eclair and Le Café

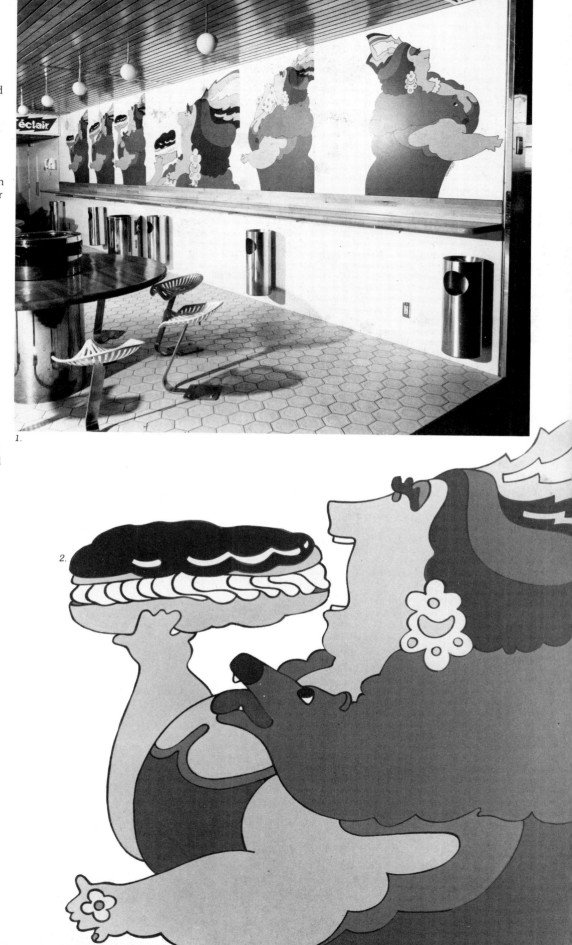

1.

2.

1. Bright mural, simple materials, tractor seats in L'Eclair restaurant.
2. Detail from the mural: an endangered éclair.

Campagne are inexpensive restaurants, and their graphics have an appropriately modest air. Imperfections (such as a wall thermostat in the middle of an onion) seem to be minor. In general, the two environments achieve their effects not with expense, but with imagination and freshness: they successfuly suggest that the same characteristics are true of food. What more could a restaurateur ask?

3.

4.

3. On one wall of Le Café Campagne, a photomural of giant onions...
4, 6....and on the other wall, apples.
5. Full view of the L'Eclair wall.

Client: Cara Operations
Design firm: Jacques Guillon/ Designers Inc., Montreal
Designers: Frederic Metz, Project Designer; Laurent Marquart, Consulting Partner; Patricia Moroz, Interior Project Designer
Architect: PGL Architects
Fabricator: Binette & Assoc. (Café Campagne); André Shirmer (L'Eclair)

3.

British airways
Air France
Royal Air Maroc
Iberia
Sabena
Nordair
Alitalia
Lufthansa

Ai
Cze
Gene

TAXI

4.

Olympic
Wardair

Départs des vols
Flight departures

Aviation Services

5.

British airways
BA 648 Prestwick/Manchester

British airways
BA 600 Londres/London

BA 600 Londres/London

BA Londres

British

British

6.

1. Bilingual signs, black on yellow.
2, 4. Directional symbols have a
   white ground for maximum
   visibility.
3. Construction detail: Fiberglas
   neatly fit into a metal frame.
5, 6. Allowance for individuality in
   airline identification.

8.

9.

10.

11.

7. Parking area signing is similar in
character, bolder in size.
8-11. Variety of placements and
shapes, but uniformity of style.

Client: New Montreal International
Airport Project Office, Ministry of
Transport, Canada
Design firm: Jacques
Guillon/Designers Inc., Montreal
Designers: Laurent Marquart,
Partner-in-Charge; Morley L. Smith,
Jr., Consulting Partner; Robert Ethier,
Project Graphic Designer; Guy
Demers, Pierre Tardif, Industrial
Designers
Architect: PGL Architects
Fabricator: Simpsons Contract
Division

7.

Milwaukee's Summerfest is an annual ten-day event on the shore of Lake Michigan, with music, theater, sports, folk dancing, ethnic foods, and—by no means least important—the famous Milwaukee beers. Local artists John Reiss and Lois Ehlert were asked to design the graphics for the festival, but with requirements for unusual flexibility and with the restrictions inherent in a low budget and in the fact that much of the work was to be executed by Summerfest's own work crew (energetic, but hardly professional sign fabricators). To every extent possible, Reiss and Ehlert have designed elements not just suitable for one summer but adaptable for many years of re-use. They include:

First, a series of "information towers" imaginatively constructed of stacked cubes. Each cube is a 3′ module with faces of Duraply plywood, and as many as six are stacked together, forming towers 18′ high. The 3′ size was felt to be the maximum that could be easily handled by one person. These cubes are highly adaptable: they can be stacked in many different combinations, turned to face different directions, or have some of their surfaces completely revamped when necessary.

Second, an existing stage, previously neglected in regard to its appearance and used primarily for concerts by local rock groups, was painted in a dynamic chevron design. Its colors were kept relatively dark, allowing spotlighted

1.

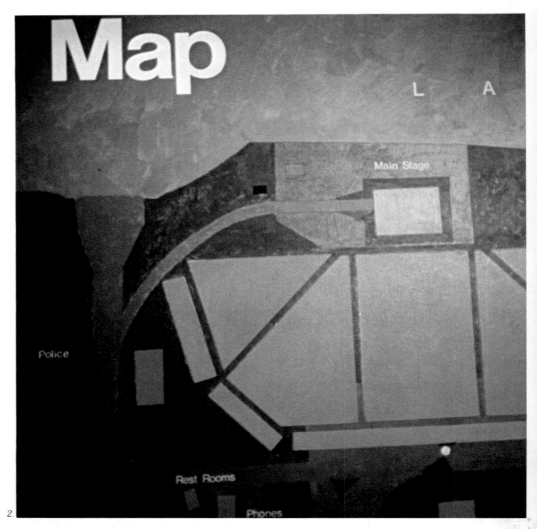

2.

1, 2. Distant and detail views of one of the site maps, designed like all the Summerfest graphics with annual alterations in mind.
3. A calendar of events for the stage.
4. The chevron backdrop of the stage.
5. Flexible "information towers" built of stacked plywood cubes.

3.

4.

5.

performers to appear as
bright as possible against the
background. Reiss and Ehlert
suggest that the color of the
brightest stripes be altered
every year for visual variety.

Third, maps of the entire
Summerfest site on 4′ by 8′
plywood panels that can be
mounted on 4′ by 4′ posts or
directly on the supports of the
bleachers. In bright, but not
quite primary colors (selected
as being unlikely to be
confused with the colors of
merchandising signs of nearby
food and beverage vendors),
the maps are coded to
indicate different features:
food facilities are red-purple;
rest rooms, yellow-green;
entertainment areas, golden
yellow. The Summerfest
grounds' temporary as well as
permanent buildings are all
located on the maps; even
tents are shown. But, by
touching up with a bit of
plastic paint, these indications
can easily be changed from
year to year. The maps'
surfaces are protected by
sheets of Lexan plastic.

As a guide for the addition
of new stacking cubes, or
new signs of any kind, Reiss
and Ehlert have prescribed
strict rules for the size and
placement of lettering.
Standard letters for
Summerfest are white, 3′
high, and in Helvetica
typeface; they were printed
on applicator tape by
Architectural Signing of
Marina Del Rey, California;
and actual application of
letters from tape to painted
plywood was made—largely
in Reiss' own office—by the
Summerfest crew and a work
force of art students.

6. *"Information towers."*

Client: Milwaukee World Festival,
Inc.
Designers: John Reiss, Chief; Lois
Ehlert, Associate
Fabricator: Architectural Signing
Other consultants: City of
Milwaukee Engineers

This environmental graphics program for a chain of sporting goods stores grew out of a more conventional graphics program executed four years ago. Two young Kansas City entrepreneurs, Michael McGrannahan and Bitsy Cavanaugh, had founded a corporation for the importing and distribution of European and Japanese bicycles, and had commissioned Richard Lucente to design a symbol for their stationery and business cards. Based on a side view of a bicycle, it seemed successful, and as the corporation and its affiliated retail outlets grew, it was applied and adapted, "without," as Lucente says, "the luxury of a long-range plan."

When asked to re-use the symbol in a Yellow Pages ad, Lucente decided, and his clients agreed, that it was time for a less conventional image; thus, the rather abstract frontal view of a cyclist wearing competition headgear.

In 1974, the still-growing Ride-On chain held its first outdoor advertising campaign, and for it Lucente made a further adaptation of his symbol: repetitions with tonal gradations. The next year brought a further commission —the design and execution of graphics on a large van that was to be used as a mobile bike repair unit and consequently as a mobile billboard. Like all the previous work, the van was designed in black, gray, and white. It was followed by the exterior design of a Ride-On branch in Lawrence, Kansas, and for this store, Lucente added color. In graduated hues of blues and oranges, there were 14 10'-high cyclist symbols, all painted for a budget of $1000. Applied lettering (in white, so as not to be lost among the cyclists) was constructed of epoxy-coated masonite.

Ride-On has become a very popular bicycle dealer in the Kansas City area, and its symbol and its colors are now universally recognized. There has even been a change from Ride-On Bicycles to Ride-On Outdoor Sports, an expansion of merchandise to include hiking and tennis equipment (and requiring additional symbol designs).

Lucente's latest work for Ride-On is a new store facade and interior in the Oak Park Mall of suburban Overland Park, Kansas. For the 2800-sq. ft. store, he was given a budget of $30,000 and a time schedule—for both designing and building—of 90 days. Exterior graphics, featuring an 8'-high version of the now-familiar cyclist, were painted with gloss enamel on plastic laminate; lettering on the 3' by 30' sign band above is routed out of the plastic, backed with white acrylic, and—as required by the shopping center—internally illuminated. All other lettering is adhesive-backed vinyl.

The jury had a few reservations about Ride-On's graphics. Some thought that the symbol repetitions were at times *too* repetitive: some thought the color gradations were confusing when applied to a heavily textured brick surface. But there was much general admiration, particularly for the treatment of the mobile unit. Applied to the smooth white surface of the van, the symbols are easily read, the sense of movement appropriate, and the total effect striking.

1.

1. *The typical Ride-On logo: superimposed bikes in various colors.*

2.

2. In a suburban shopping mall, the entrance to a typical Ride-On outlet.
3. Beginning as bicycle importers, the company now sells equipment for tennis and other sports.
4. Ride-On's van, a mobile bicycle repair unit, is also a striking advertising billboard that travels through the whole Kansas City area.
5. Above a suburban outlet, the symbol at billboard scale.

3.

4.

Clients: Michael McGrannahan,
Bitsy Cavanaugh
Designer: Richard Lucente

5.

National Air and Space Museum

The work by HOK/Graphics (a branch of Hellmuth, Obata & Kassabaum, Architects) for the Smithsonian Institution's new National Air and Space Museum, itself designed by HOK and now handsomely flanking the Washington Mall, is one of the most varied in scope of all this year's Casebook selections.

It varies from a myriad of fittingly unobtrusive details (door signs, for example, and elevator indicators) to at least one feature which, uncharacteristically, smacks of official pomposity and even, just a bit, of corn (the 6'-diameter bronze "compass rose" embedded in the floor) to a number of unusual graphic elements striking in both size and style.

That style is perhaps most impressively demonstrated in areas where the most decorative liberties have been taken. Two of these are the concrete block walls of a potentially dreary 500-car underground garage and the glass screens which modulate the space of the museum's large third-floor dining area. In both these cases, the graphics are adapted from photographs or engravings of man's early attempts at flight, some of them, such as The Spirit of St. Louis, successful attempts, some, such as an elaborate apparatus powered by a swarm of harnessed birds, or a group of winged men holding umbrellas, rather more fantastic, but all of them entertaining. The dining room murals are silkscreened directly on the glass; the garage murals are painted on

1.

2.

Photos: Barbara Martin (Fig. 1), Kiku Obata (Figs. 2, 3)

3.

1-3. New National Air and Space Museum building, facing the National Gallery of Art directly across the Mall, is strong and appropriately dignified. Graphics, both inside and out, share that same character.

x

29/Environmental Graphics

the block walls. (The jury had some doubt here about long-range maintenance: the present murals are attractively precise in outline, but how easily could that precision be kept when time came for repainting the wall? Very easily, says HOK's Charles Reay: the murals, all in a single color only, are applied in a follow-the-dots technique commonly used for billboard display painting, and the museum has kept the original perforated templates for just such future use.)

For the more conventional signing elements of the program, the HOK designers have rightly felt that appropriate character was as important a consideration as instant readability, so Craw Clarendon typeface was chosen in preference to Helvetica. Major aluminum and Plexiglas signs, spanning gallery entrances, are not only in English, but also—at smaller size—in French, Spanish, German, and Japanese. This multilingual presentation aids foreign visitors, obviously, but even for those who read only English, it reinforces an impression of the worldwide significance of the exhibits housed here.

Also in all five languages throughout the building are internally illuminated directories, combining diagrammatic floor plans with changeable photographs of major exhibits for quick orientation. All these graphic elements were evaluated by HOK not only on the basis of immediate usefulness and original cost, but also

4.

5.

6.

4, 5. Graphics details are thoughtful and generally unobtrusive.
6. On a distant column is one of the museum's helpful diagrammatic floor plans directing visitors to exhibits.
7. Close-up of diagrammatic floor plan.
8. Mural based on engraving of "Spirit of St. Louis" in the museum's underground garage.
9, 10. In the third-floor dining room, delightful murals show man's early attempts at flight.

8.

9.

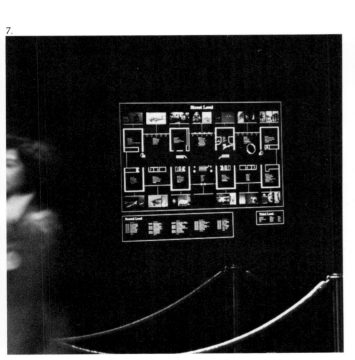
7.

10.

Photos: Kiku Obata (Figs. 4, 5, 7, 9, 10), Barbara Martin (Figs. 6, 8) (considering provisions for flexibility) on the basis of projected total cost after ten years. Many elements here, though initially costly, have wisely been chosen for long-range savings.

The Air and Space Museum is one of Washington's most important new buildings, both because of its collection and because of its absolutely critical location, facing the Mall near the Capitol and directly opposite the National Gallery of Art. It is a pleasure to see HOK's architecture working so effectively in this location. And it is a further pleasure, considering the complexity and changeability of the building's contents, to see the whole ensemble so well enhanced by its graphics.

Photos: Kiku Obata

11

Client: General Services Administration (owner); National Air and Space Museum, Smithsonian Institution (user)
Design firm: HOK/Graphics, St. Louis
Designers: Paul J. Henderson, Charles P. Reay
Architect: Hellmuth, Obata, Kassabaum
Fabricator: Cummings, Inc.

National Air and Space Museum
← Service Entry, No Automobiles
Two Way Traffic

Gallery 114
Space Hall
Salle de l'espace
Sala del Espacio
Ausstellungshalle für
Raumfahrzeuge
宇宙館

Gallery 110   Satellites   Satellites
Satélites
Satelliten
人工衛星

11. Bronze ''compass rose,'' 6' in diameter, imbedded in floor.
12. Exterior directional sign.
13, 14. Exhibit captions are written in five languages.

Canadian National Signing Program

The use of symbols to replace words is likely to be forever controversial (has there ever been a symbol *everybody* understood?). But in Canada, symbols have become a way of quieting controversy.

Although two-thirds of Canada's population speaks only English, French has been the official language of the eastern province of Quebec, Canada's largest province, since 1974. Disputes between English and French language groups have been frequent and emotional, and there is now a network of hotly contested laws regulating the language of classrooms and private businesses.

Signs in both languages are obviously necessary, but only bring up a further difficulty: Which language comes first? In the new nationwide signing program designed by Hunter Straker Templeton Ltd., of Toronto, for the Canadian Department of Public Works, French is to have the honored place on the left side of each sign in areas with a French-speaking majority; English will be on the left in other areas.

With words so likely to stir intranational animosity, symbols become unusually attractive, and it should not surprise us that Hunter Straker Templeton have recommended signing that depends on glyphs as much as possible. With 120 symbols already accepted as standard, and with work progressing on another 60 to be added, the Canadian system must be one of the most extensive—if not *the* most extensive— anywhere. All this is

1.

1. *Typing pool glyph.*
2. *Telephone glyph.*
3. *Drinking water glyph.*

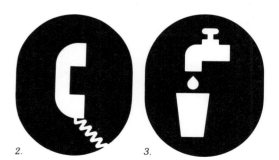

2.   3.

admirably well organized for use on signs limited to a single shape, two different sizes (5⅞" high and 11" high), and three different color combinations (white figures on a blue background for "permissive" information, black on yellow for warnings, and white on red for fire safety messages and strict prohibitions). All this is also admirably well outlined and presented in easily understood guides (bilingual, of course) to the symbols and signs.

There is, however, a danger inherent in the program's very thoroughness. No matter how well designed a symbol may be, it still depends to some extent on viewer familiarity for its recognition. The Canadians have been given a great

many symbols with which to become familiar, and some of those symbols—the one for "rest area," for example, or the one for "typing pool"— are not clear to everyone seeing them for the first time.

A further, unexpected complication, discovered during Hunter Straker Templeton's testing of the first 25 symbols, is that French-speaking and English-speaking groups do not always respond to symbols in the same way. This suggests any number of speculations on the esoteric nature of visual communication, and indicates just how complicated the use of symbols really is. Perhaps, even, that typing pool symbol would seem perfectly obvious if our native language were French.

4. A. Men's washroom, women's washroom, janitor's room, men at work, cloak room, electrical outlet, picnic, mail receiver. B. Lecture room, board room, for handicapped, no smoking, parking, lockers, down left, philately. C. Restaurant, cafeteria, coffee shop, cashier, no food or beverages, refreshments, dogs prohibited, money order. D. Painters, plumbers, electricians, carpenters, boiler plant, battery room, laboratory, shower. E. Fan room, mechanical room, stationery, lost and found, typing pool, library, photo equipment, theater. F. Bus loading zone, buses, cars only, no cars, taxi, no trucks, bicycles, no bicycles. G. Anchorage, sailing, marina, boating, boat launching, canoeing, boat tie up, row boating. H. Skiing, cross country, skating, hockey prohibited, hunting, no hunting, swimming, diving. I. Camping, firewood, campfires, no campfires, drinking water, portage, fishing, no fishing.
5-12. Glyphs in use, combined with other glyphs, with text or alone.

Client: Public Works Canada
Design firm: Hunter Straker Templeton, Ltd., Toronto

5.

6.

7.

8.

9.

10.

11.

12.

Washington Metro Maps

"Terrifying," one judge said of the prospect of a commission such as this one: the design of all neighborhood maps and a general system map for the Metro, Washington, D.C.'s new subway system.

Metro's first section, 4.5 miles of track with six stations, opened in March, 1976; a second increment, with 24 more stations, is scheduled to open in April, 1977; and when the entire system is completed (1982 is the date planned), it will have 82 stations and 100 miles of track, extending beyond District boundaries into suburban Maryland and Virginia.

If New York designers Wyman and Cannan felt terror at such a mapping job, it doesn't show. In the graphics produced, an air of clear-headed composure prevails.

The maps were produced within the constraint of a general color coding previously prescribed for the entire system by Unimark International (designers of Metro's symbol and all other graphics excluding the maps), giving each of the system's five lines of track its own color. Unimark had also prescribed Helvetica Medium typeface for the system.

A further constraint was that the positioning and size of all map displays in the stations and trains were dictated by the Washington Metropolitan Area Transit Authority. Flexibility was a requirement, too: maps had to be adaptable to reflect current realities at each stage

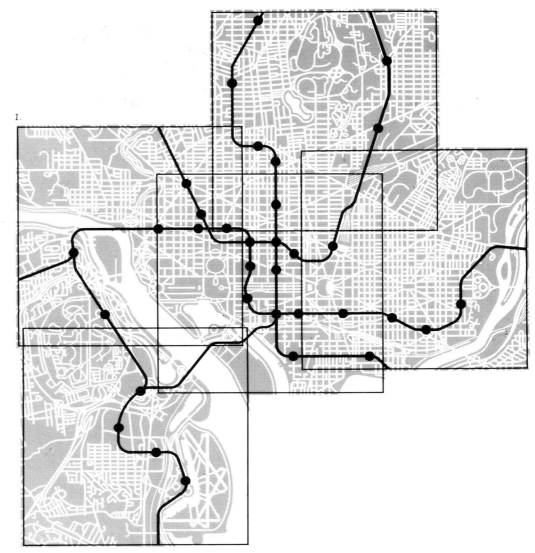

1.

2.

Client: Washington Metropolitan Area Transit Authority
Design firm: Wyman and Cannan Co., New York
Designers: Lance Wyman, Bill Cannan, Brian Flahive, Steve Harding
Architect: Harry Weese Associates
Fabricator: Timsco
Consultant: Judith Harkinson (map data)

of the system's growth. A design budget of $60,000 and a time schedule of 18 months were allowed.

Wyman and Cannan produced art, specifications, and contract documents for a number of different maps. In the stations, there are pairs of back-illuminated maps 3' wide and 4' high, silkscreened on sheets of translucent styrene. One of each pair is a map of the entire system, with estimated travel times to all its possible destinations, and with a table of fares (a graduated fare scale will be introduced when the second increment of stations is opened). The other is a map of the particular three-mile-square neighborhood around each station, with an index locating landmarks, parks, government buildings and tourist attractions.

In addition, 32"-square opaque system maps in offset lithography are placed on the trains themselves. Finally, there are small handout folders with system maps, fare and time data, and—to help subsidize production costs—one advertising panel on the back of each folder.

The overall-system maps, whether illuminated or opaque, suffer the difficulty common to all such maps: a conflict of scale between the underground express system and the much more finely-grained detail of surface geography. Allowing the underground pattern to read boldly and clearly necessitates considerable abstraction and oversimplification of the surface level, and this can seem disorientingly surreal to those looking for the familiar shapes of the tidal basin or the wiggles in the Potomac shoreline. And so the second map of each pair, with all the city's wiggles and idiosyncrasies intact, is particularly important for user orientation.

Wyman and Cannan retained Judith Harkinson as a consultant to conduct research on the data each neighborhood map should show, and local community and planning groups were also asked to advise. Approximate walking distances from the Metro station to the features shown on the map can be judged by means of concentric rings representing increments of one-eighth-mile distances (or about a five-minute walk) from the station. Five slightly overlapping neighborhood maps cover the area served by the system's first six stations; when all stations are open, 27 such maps will be needed.

On the overall-maps, stations in service are shown as black circles, future stations as white circles. Maps can thus easily be kept current simply by overprinting black circles on white ones as the system grows.

1. Washington Metro map.
2. Foldout pamphlet shows map, time schedule and fare rate.
3. Maps show entire Metro system area immediately surrounding station.

World Trade Center Observation Deck

Warren Platner Associates were given no specific instructions for the design of this observation level. What they were given instead were several unique opportunities and demands: an acre of space 107 floors in the air over the tip of Manhattan, the expectation of between two and three million visitors a year, and the request by the World Trade Center for the best such facility in the world.

After extensive research on the highest floor of the man-made world, the Platner office concluded that most observation areas treat their visitors quite perfunctorily. In contrast, they suggested some positive amenities: First, because most tourists are on their feet much of the time, there should be places to sit. Second, even those who do want to stand and walk should be as comfortable as possible. Third, because everyone will want an unobstructed view, there should be several tiers of possible viewing stations. Fourth, for those (such as busloads of schoolchildren who may have planned the outing for months) who may arrive when the view is completely fogged in, there should be something else to see as well. And fifth, the design should include some information to viewers about just what it is they're viewing.

The actual design of the information diagrams (labeled perspective sketches on the glass, spaced about 10 feet apart and identifying prominent features of the actual views), as well as the design and installation of the

1.

Photos: Alexandre Georges

2.

1. Seating and standing arrangements
   offer an unusual number of visitors
   simultaneous, but unobstructed,
   views.
2. Line drawings on the windows
   correspond to actual views, and
   identify major points of interest.

exhibition encircling the building's core (dealing with the history of world trade, and presenting, in an agreeable and intriguing jumble, such facts as that the dromedary camel has one hump), were the work of Milton Glaser, Inc., brought into the job as consultants at Platner's suggestion.

But the conception of the deck and many of its critical details are Platner's. Perhaps the most critical of all of these is the decision to raise the floor level by about two feet, providing sub-floor benches for those who want to press their noses right against the glass. Because of the level change, angled views downward are still unobscured for those behind them. Platner estimates that seating is available for a thousand people at a time. A further amenity, for those who just want to comfortably slouch, is a series of leaning rails a few feet back from the glass. These rails, as open as safety allows, are of nylon-coated steel.

Even those who just want to stroll about have been considered—the floor is cushioned with embossed rubber flooring. And, properly focusing attention on the view or (in cloudy weather) the exhibit, everything else is colored a soft warm gray.

At the core of the square floor, inside the exhibit walls, are rest rooms, a concession area, a snack bar and a gift shop.

The construction budget, assigned in 1970, was $1,250,000—a sum adhered to despite inflation. As a result, some of Platner's ideas remain unbuilt. There is, for example, no finished ceiling, just exposed I-beams with their sprayed-on insulation. While this is, in a way, a welcome contrast to the lavender vulgarity of the lobby spaces far below, Platner's concept of a ceiling of mirror-polished stainless steel, making a view upward really a duplication of the great view downward, will undoubtedly be spectacular when and if it is installed.

3.

3. More seating at the Observation Deck.
4. View from the top.

4.

Client: World Trade Center of New York, The Port Authority of New York and New Jersey
Design firm: Warren Platner Associates, Architects, New Haven, CT
Architect: Minoru Yamasaki & Associates
Consultants: Milton Glaser, Inc., Exhibition Design; Skilling, Helle, Christiansen, Robertson, Structural Engineers; Jaros, Baum & Bolles, Mechanical Engineers; Emery Roth & Sons, Consulting Architects
Fabricator: Bristol Construction

Photos: Alexandre Georges

Knoxville
Zoological Park

Some graphics programs supplement words with pictographs for the benefit of people who speak several languages; this one, developed for Knoxville's Zoological Park, employs the visual elements for those who may not read at all—young children.

The program, almost four years in development, was conceived by Birney Hand, an architect with GSW Architecture and Planning when work was first begun, who subsequently opened his own architectural firm, Atelier 105, as well as a graphic design office, Handprints (this, with his wife Karen), during design execution and implementation.

In 1972, the Knoxville Zoo had been little more than an animal prison, containing, among other beasts, an unfortunately ravenous elephant whose appetite was out of all proportion to the city budget. Now, with new funds and revamped into a true zoological park, it is a considerate home for the animals and a popular place indeed for human visitors.

Especially young ones. The 16"-square animal identification signs, which form the core of the facility's graphics program, are considerately placed for these visitors, with the units' bottom edge's positioned only 18" above the ground. Sign faces, however, are tilted back 30 degrees from the vertical so that information is also quite easily seen by a 6'-tall adult. This tilt, incidentally, also lets rainwater run easily off the face of the sign, which is a

1. Hippos wade behind a sign that describes their tastes and habitats.
2. Pictograph for a bear.

1.

2.

⅛"-thick sheet of non-glare Plexiglas over the silkscreened art. The supporting standard for each sign is of self-oxidizing steel, the color and texture of which are compatible with other "earthy" materials specified for the zoo.

What's more important, of course, are the designs of the signs themselves. The most prominent feature of each sign is an easily recognized symbol of a particular animal species. After some unsuccessful work with other artists, the Hands commissioned Lois Ehlert, a children's book illustrator from Milwaukee, to design these symbols. Abstract as they are, Ehlert's animals retain a great many endearing idiosyncrasies. If her timber wolf looks a bit forlorn, if her bears' noses seem a bit long, and if her African elephant reminds us just a bit of Babar—well, it is these features which help give the symbols so much personality.

The signs don't provide just animal identification; listed for each species are an identification of its food, its types of habitat, and the range of its natural location. This information is given in both words and symbols.

Colored signs were originally planned, with the color for an animal type keyed to the color used on the walls of a particular section of zoo buildings. In practice, however, the animals have proved to be so transient—being moved so often from one section to another—that the colors have been abandoned in favor of white symbols and lettering on a black ground.

The most serious complication faced by the designers during their work was a budget crisis that threatened to eliminate the program completely. Municipal bonds originally furnished $3.5 million for the zoo's entire rehabilitation, including architectural and engineering work as well as graphics, for which $20,000 had been budgeted. But before the first sign was fabricated, all the funds had already been spent.

The Hands were disappointed but persistent; they approached zoo officials with the proposal that Handprints itself market the signs, attempting to get them paid for by individuals and businesses on a donor basis. The effort was successful; every sign in the program was completed, with the only change necessary being an additional copy line not originally planned, identifying each unit's donor.

This unusual donor system is felt, by the Hands, to have greatly increased a sense of community participation in the zoo. Most satisfying, they add, has been the eager participation of Knoxville schoolchildren; one group of youngsters raised money to sponsor a sign for an area known as the "petting zoo," where tame animals are allowed to run freely and be touched by children. A future addition planned for this area will be signs in Braille, perhaps even with a few feathers or pieces of fur attached, so that the blind

3.

BALD EAGLE

FOOD

HABITAT

RANGE

southeast north america

graphics donated by:
members of tenn. chapter 99's
intl. org. of women pilots
handprints 1975

4.

AFRICAN ELEPHANT

FOOD

HABITAT

RANGE

africa

animal donated by:
shoney's

handprints 1975

3. *Bald eagle pictograph.*
4. *Elephant pictograph.*
5. *Signs are low for children, but tilted for easy adult reading, too.*

GRIZZLY BEAR

AFRICAN LION

can identify animals by touch.

The program's success has not been confined to Knoxville. The Hands have presented it to an International Zoological Society convention in Calgary, Canada, and, with the English words translated into Chinese, the signs have been adapted for use by the Kaoshiung Zoological Park in Taiwan.

7.

COUGAR

FOOD

HABITAT

RANGE

north & south america

graphics donated by:
clayton lincoln, mercury inc.

6.

8.

非 洲 獅

嗜食

棲息

產地

非洲

9.

6. Deer pictograph.
7. Zoo graphics as they appear in English.
8. A Chinese version.
9. Some of the symbols for habitats, food supplies, native continents, and for the animals themselves.
10. Sign in place at the eagle cage.

Client: Knoxville Zoological Park
Design firm: Handprints, Knoxville, TN
Designer: Birney Hand
Illustrator: Lois Ehlert
Architect: GSW Architecture & Planning
Fabricator: APCO Graphics
Other consultants: Jim Haggerty—Plastics Design & Sales

Sometimes an environment is most successful when made to seem uncharacteristic, unexpected, or even inappropriate. A hospital is such a place. By nature a source of anxiety and even fear, it is yet possible to give the building a character which is—visually, at least—pleasant, even jolly. That was the aim here.

The location is a major new expansion to the existing Our Lady of Lourdes Hospital in Camden, New Jersey. Brought into the job when the building was already under construction, New York designer Al Corchia had 60 days to create the graphics, and he began working at once with hospital administrator Sister Elizabeth Coury. It was Sister Elizabeth who first insisted that the interiors have a cheerful atmosphere. Everyone agreed, but it was obvious that such an effect would not likely be achieved with signing alone; something much more potent would be needed.

In Corchia's solution, the first object seen upon entering the new wing is a crucifix. While it is clearly—though not too literally—just that, and while it retains a fitting degree of dignity, the crucifix is nevertheless freshly designed and brightly presented (in two colors of porcelainized steel), implying that more felicitous design may be just around the corner.

Indeed it is. The major impact of this graphics program comes from a series of large murals painted directly on the walls of the

1.

2.

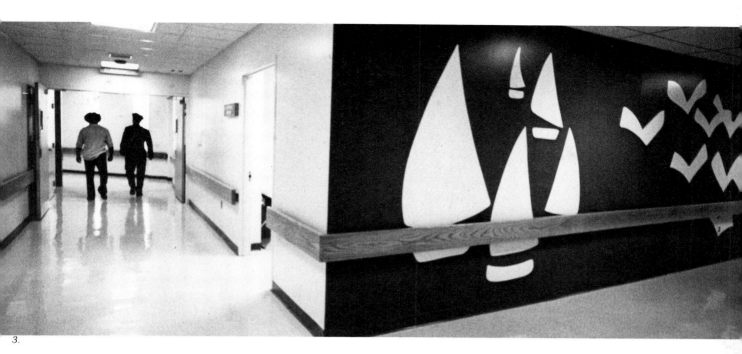

3.

4.

1. At hospital entrance, an abstract crucifix.
2. On ground floor, "flower" theme is introduced on directories.
3. "Water" mural fits theme of first floor.
4. Ground floor "flower" mural.

hospital's public spaces (its corridors, waiting areas, exercise rooms, and cafeteria). In colors that are bright but not harsh, these murals are all highly stylized abstractions from nature. They are not random in location, but are placed in accordance with an organizational scheme which assigns each floor a specific symbol and color scheme, and which is an aid in floor identification and orientation. The cellar floor, partly used for storage, has as its appropriate symbol an acorn. The ground floor, immediately above, has murals based on flowers. The theme of the first floor is water; of the second floor, trees; of the third (top) floor, sun.

In addition to the murals, there are, of course, more conventional graphics: signs on all room doors, and the usual array of labels and directional signs. These graphics are constructed primarily of melamine, a material chosen because it is easy to maintain, is available in a wide range of colors, and has a white core. Colors were chosen to relate to each floor's murals, and letters and symbols were sandblasted through the colored surface to expose the core.

Another pleasant touch is that these signs have been framed in oak. The frames give the signs depth, substance, and some additional warmth, and the oak was chosen to match the handrails and other pieces of wood trim specified by the architects.

5.

6.

5. Ground floor directional signs.
6. Cafeteria.
7. Oak chair rail protects mural.
8. Directory keys floors to symbols.

7.

8.

Directory

Third Floor Surgery

Second Floor Inpatient

First Floor
Physical Therapy
Occupational Therapy
Pulmonary Therapy
Hearing and Speech
Social Service
EKG EMG EEG

Ground Floor
Emergency
Ambulatory Care
Purchasing
Employee's Dining

R·G36 Waiting Room

Client: Our Lady of Lourdes Hospital
Design firm: Al Corchia, Inc., New York
Designers: Al Corchia, Albert Sibley
Architect: The Eggers Partnership
Associate architect: Paul W. Reilly
Fabricators: The Other Sign Company (signing); County Neon Sign Corp. (crucifix)

GAF Corporate Headquarters

For the design of its own office facilities in Wayne, New Jersey, the GAF Corporation turned to its own Design Services branch, headed by Paul Miller, and to the interior design firm of Stockman and Manners.

The bulk of their efforts concentrated on the enlivening of office work space. As the space existed, it was filled with cubicles formed by a modular wall system, admirably flexible but, the designers thought, overly bland and repetitive; people felt dehumanized working in a sterile 5 by 5 modular unit.

Their remedy was to paint the white partitions in spectrum colors of red, orange, yellow, green, blue and violet. Building core walls and even furniture were in colors to match. (A mild cavil is that although some workers may indeed feel dehumanized in a white grid, some others may feel thoroughly raped to be caged in walls of spectrum violet.) More imaginative and perhaps more genuinely humanizing was the use, in many of the building's windowless office spaces, of a series of large landscape photographs of the Delaware Water Gap region by photographer Elliot Kaufman.

In addition to these general office spaces, the work included the reception area and the employee cafeteria. In the reception area, eveything was kept pleasantly simple, with emphatic focus on a single bold element: an 8'-wide neon version of the newly designed GAF corporate logo, a crisp and

1.

2.

attractive graphic device of slightly-run-together Helvetica letters. The neon panel not only establishes the character of the reception area, but, seen from outside the building—perhaps even from outside the state—it also clearly marks the building entrance.

In the cafeteria, the existing fluorescent lighting (which, in its non-color-corrected versions, can make food look quite unpalatable) was warmed by 1′ by 4′ red acrylic baffles hung from the ceiling fixtures. The baffles effectively alter the room's ambient light, as well as limit direct views of the light sources. The food looks better, too.

4.

1. The reception area is brightened and unmistakably identified by a giant neon version of the GAF logo.
2, 3. Corporate ID on the GAF trucks.
4. Company cafeteria has quieter sound, more indirect and warmer lighting due to a pattern of hanging baffles.

5.

6.

Client: Design Services, GAF Corp.
Design firm: Stockman and Manners, New York
Designers: Paul D. Miller—GAF; Judith Stockman—Stockman and Manners
Fabricator: Structural Displays Co.
Other consultants: West Side Sign Co. (neon); Elliot Kaufman (photography)

7.

8.

9.

10.

5, 6. Colors, logo and materials are consistent throughout the GAF offices.
7. Manual specifies graphic standards.
8. Exterior sign.
9, 10. Prominent among the wall treatments is a series of landscape murals by photographer Eliot Kaufman.

In and around Indianapolis there is a prototype cluster of six quick-copy centers serving local architects, accountants, engineers, and others, called Print Express. The centers offer quick Diazo prints, color printing, microfilming, cameras, stationery, art and drafting supplies, and a range of GAF paper and film products.

The first center constructed was studied carefully for any design flaws; a manual prescribing the parameters for further installations was written. The next five centers were installed by the local managers themselves, following the manual.

Flexibility to meet varied conditions was obviously necessary, and both tight budgets and tight time schedules were anticipated. A basic decision was to rely on a commercially available wire shelf system ("Erecta" by Metropolitan Wire goods), requiring no fasteners (the pieces can be knocked together with a rubber mallet) and serving as both storage and retail display units. Most of the 7′-high units have one side closed by a panel of bright red ⅛″ Plexiglas. Silkscreened to these panels at an angle are general terms describing the shelved products, and this lettering is superimposed on a 2½″ white grid. The grid has appropriate connotations of modularity, precision, and graphs of all sorts. The angling of the lettering is due to...well, perhaps just because it looks rather jaunty that way. The Helvetica Bold typeface is a GAF Corporation standard, as

is the red color.

Success of the six initial prototype shops has led to a continuation of the program, still following the original manual, at 12 more locations in the U.S. and at additional centers in England, Belgium, and Australia.

1, 2. Red grid design is quickly identifiable; lighting and displays are thoroughly flexible at GAF Print Express.

1.

Logan Airport

Graphics programs of some types are successful in inverse proportion to their "visualness." The directional signs of a large airport complex, for example, are meant to direct people to gates, to taxis, or to baggage, not to attract attention to themselves (except that they must, of course, be readable and quickly recognized as signs). The graphics by Page, Arbitrio & Resen for the new South Terminal at Boston's Logan Airport, judged by such a standard, are highly successful. If they lack the flair or the arresting appearance of some of the other graphics programs shown here, that lack is intentional and proper.

The designers were retained by the terminal's architects, John Carl Warnecke and Associates and Desmond & Lord, Inc., but they were ultimately responsible to the Massachusetts Port Authority. The scope of the work included all public (non-tenant) space signing, on-site roadway signs, exterior gate signs, and garage signs. Lettering is silkscreened on aluminum panels with a baked enamel finish. For the most part, lettering is black on a white ground. For interior signs, white letters on a dark brown or black background were also suggested, but these alternatives were rejected as incompatible with the architecture.

An exception to the severely businesslike color scheme is in the garage and along the roofed approach

1.

2.

1, 2. Legibility without ostentation is the key to the complex signing program for Boston's new south terminal.

road, where color coding has been skillfully used. Where parallel overhead beams have prevented the visibility needed for large lettering sizes, the needed impact has been achieved with the repetition of identical small signs.

Two years were allocated for the design work, and final decisions were based on study models, full-size mock-ups, and ''on location'' tests.

3-9. In elevators, on directional signs, and on parking levels, floors are color-coded. A few signs have been supplemented with pictorial symbols, but everything fussy or unnecessary has been pared away.

3.

5.

Client: Massachusetts Port Authority
Design firm: Page, Arbitrio & Resen, New York
Designer: Ken Resen
Architects: John Carl Warnecke and Associates; Desmond & Lord, Inc.
Fabricator: Donnelly Electric Sign Co.

8.

6.

7.

9.

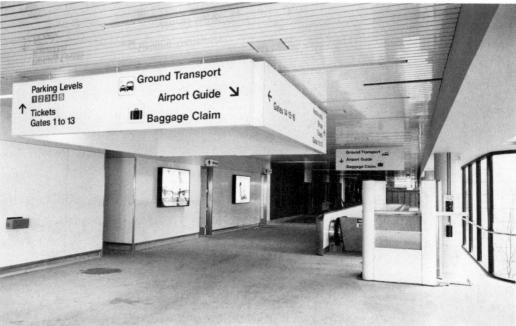

How should graphics look that identify a trail linking historic buildings and sites? They must not look the same as vehicular traffic signs, or as merchandising signs, or as bus stops, or as parking regulations. Indeed, they must not look like anything other than themselves, and it is the best measure of the success of these designs by Samuel Lebowitz that their character is so distinctive and identifiably appropriate. Seeing them for the first time, we know at once what they are.

Heritage Trail winds for approximately three miles through the financial district of lower Manhattan, its 15 identified sites including the Woolworth Building, Trinity Church, Battery Park, and the South Street Seaport. It is a trail without guides, all information and directions being provided only by the graphics program.

This program has four components. One is an identifying symbol, with stars, stripes, and the words "Heritage Trail" in an italic version of Times Roman typeface. The italic tilt and the offset relationship of letters give the symbol a directional character, and it is meant for use as a stylized arrow on markers along the trail.

Next are so-called "trailblazers." Using a vertical version of the identifying symbol, these red, white, and blue signs point the way along the trail between highlights, indicating changes in direction and reinforcing a sense of the trail's continuity. Constructed of silk-screened

1.

2.

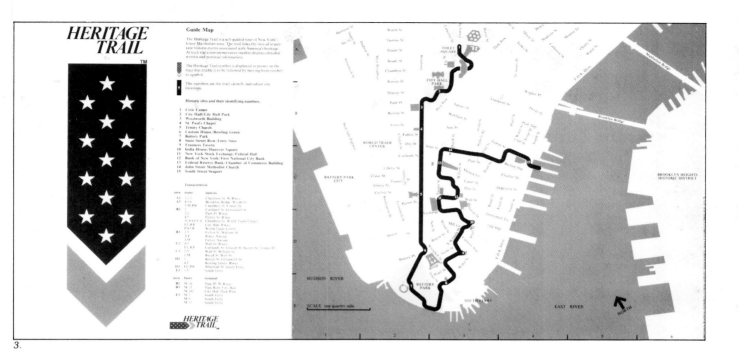

3.

1. Heritage Trail logo.
2. Three-foot-high "trailblazers" point the way along the path of historic sites.
3. Folding pocket map includes a scale plan of the area and gives public transportation information.
4. Another version of the logo.

4.

porcelain enamel on steel, they are 9″ wide, 3″ high, and mounted to existing street standards with their bottom edges nine feet above the curb, well above the obstructions of most traffic.

The third component is a booklet describing in some detail each of the points of interest seen along the trail. Public transportation information and a fold-out map of the area are included.

The final, most important and most effectively identifiable element is a series of marker signs which explain the significance of each of the trail's highlights. These signs are freestanding units 8′ high,

built of riveted aluminum box sections and bolted to steel supports that are cast into concrete foundations. The aluminum box has a dark bronze Duranodic finish, suggesting the look—without the cost—of traditional cast bronze plaques. Against this dark surface, graphics are in gold.

Unfortunately, character and legibility were not the only design considerations. Such markers—in New York, at least—are threatened by another kind of marker, the felt-tip one in the hands of the ubiquitous graffiti menace. Poster plasterers are a nuisance, too, and, of course,

there are soot and grime to be reckoned with. The graphics of the marker signs are covered with sheets of tempered glass to make the removal of dirt and graffiti as easy as possible. Along the narrow sides of the markers, and on their broad faces below the graphics, the aluminum surfaces have been prominently ribbed to discourage posters and defacement.

Texts for these signs and for the booklet have been prepared by the Lebowitz firm based on research provided by the client, with Nicholas Polites serving as consultant.

Client: The New York City Bicentennial Corporation; New York Office of Lower Manhattan Development, Technical Adviser
Design firm: Samuel Lebowitz Design and Planning, New York
Designers: Samuel Lebowitz, Peter Musgrave-Newton
Fabricators: Universal Unlimited, Inc.; Cameo, California, Metal Enameling Co.; Forrest Engraving Co., Inc.
Consulting writer: Nicholas Polites

5-7. *Marker signs in dark bronze finish give information at each significant point on the trail. On edge and base of standard, projecting ribs discourage vandalism.*

6.

7.

National Zoological Park

The Smithsonian Institution's National Zoological Park is a 165-acre facility located in Washington's Rock Creek Park. A notable feature of this sprawling establishment is the unique pedestrian walkway laid out by Frederick Law Olmsted which meanders through the areas housing animals from more than 800 species.

The Smithsonian was embarked on a farsighted zoo rehabilitation program and, as an initial step, had commissioned Washington architects Faulkner, Fryer & Vanderpool to prepare a comprehensive architectural master plan of the zoo area. With this in hand, the next objective was development of a complementary graphics master plan for the facility, to be funded jointly by the Smithsonian and the National Endowment for the Arts. New York designers Wyman and Cannan were asked to tackle this program.

If anyone still doubts that the operative definition of environmental graphics goes far beyond mere signing, Wyman and Cannan's work for the zoo should convince them; it includes not just things to read, but also things to follow, to wear (souvenir jewelry), to sit on, drink water from, and make phone calls inside of.

But the most impressive fact about this graphics program is not that it is diverse in scope, but that, despite the diversity, it is extraordinarily unified. The "O" of the zoo's new typeface is also the frame of the animal pictographs, also

1.

2.

3.

4.

5.

6.

1. Logotype for zoo.
2. Large entrance sign in model form.
3,4. Inspiration for zoo logotype: a bald eagle and her chick.
5. Necklace pendant.
6. Eagle and chick in a zoological park symbol.

7. A "totem" of appropriate animal
   symbols marks each trail through
   the zoo.
8. Totem construction is detailed.
9. Animal symbols share slightly
   rounded, slightly abstract character.
   They are bordered by the "O" of the
   zoo's typeface.

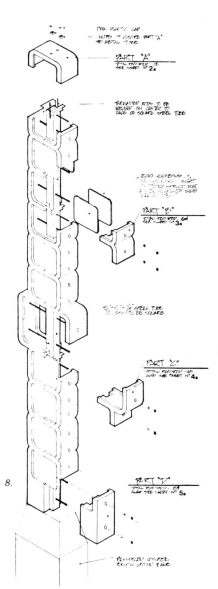

8.

7.

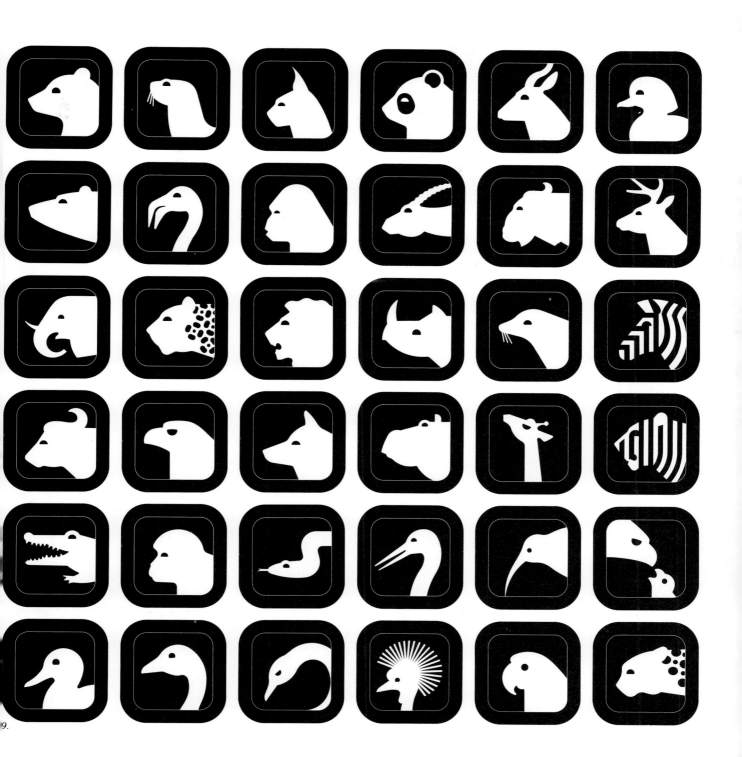

9.

the element which, when stacked, forms a directional "totem" along the Olmsted Trail, and also, slightly modified, a major feature of the seating supports, of waste receptacles, of map stands, and of information kiosks. The creation of such a distinctive and adaptable typeface is certainly a major key to the program's success.

A second key is the designers' care to relate the character of their work to the character of a zoo in a park. Except for a few bright accents, colors are muted browns and sepias; except for the dramatic (perhaps overly dramatic?) 16'-high "totems" along the main trail, all signs and equipment are as modest in scale as practicable; and the softly curved corners of the whole system—from lettering to kiosks—are comfortable and ingratiating.

A third key, of course, is hard-working professionalism (made possible, although by no means guaranteed, by a working time of two years and a design budget, including expenses, of $77,000). The graphics proposed are not by any means just drawing-board romances. In almost every case, proposed elements were not only drawn but built—in foam-core and cardboard, to be sure, but at full-size and in their proposed final locations. In many cases, these mock-ups have effected changes in the final designs: the "totem" structure, in mock-up, looked thin and was therefore strengthened; the original colors, in sunlight, looked pale and were

10.

11.

10. *Paw and claw tracks of animals and birds are used along the ground to suggest several different trails to follow.*
11. *Paw.*
12,13. *More animal tracks.*
14. *Map of zoo trails.*

12.

13.

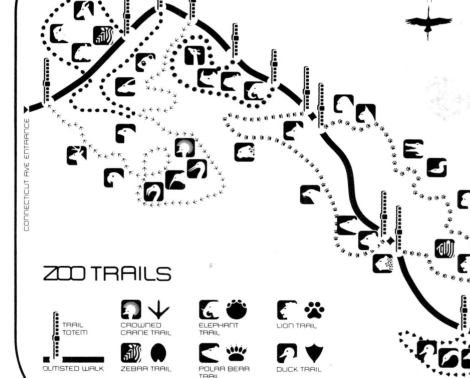

ZOO TRAILS

TRAIL TOTEM	CROWNED CRANE TRAIL	ELEPHANT TRAIL	LION TRAIL
OLMSTED WALK	ZEBRA TRAIL	POLAR BEAR TRAIL	DUCK TRAIL

CONNECTICUT AVE ENTRANCE

HARVARD ST ENTRANCE

14.

15.

16.

deepened; the original lettering looked small and was made more bold.

These adjustments have resulted in a tested guideline for all graphics and all zoo furniture which will be needed in the predictable future, a guideline to be followed by all fabricators. Material selections have been seriously examined as well—baked porcelain enamel on steel for the graphics panels, and pre-cast stone for the structural components.

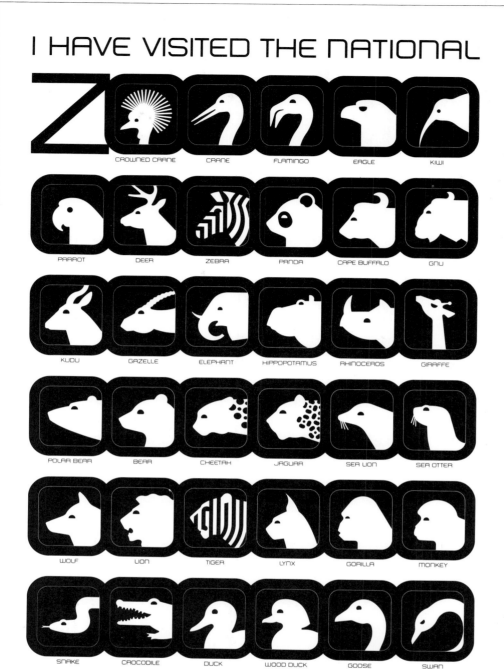

17.

18.

19.

ABCDEFG
HIJKLMN
OPQRSTU
VWXYZ
1234567
890
(!$&?'""',.;:)

20.

But the fourth key to this graphics program's appeal is charm. The "totems," the maps, the pictographs—all share in a general naturalness and warmth. For one example: trails which feature the exhibit of particular species (elephants, for instance, or cranes, or polar bears) are marked on the ground with series of circular tiles embedded in asphalt, each tile showing an appropriate animal track. Who could resist following?

15, 16. Forms of proposed benches are consistent with rounded letter forms.
17. Animal symbols identified on poster.
18, 19. Trash receptacles also serve as directors.
20. The zoo alphabet.

Client: National Zoological Park—Smithsonian Institution; National Endowment for the Arts
Design firm: Wyman and Cannan, New York
Designers: Lance Wyman, Bill Cannan, Directors; Brian Flahive, Tucker Viemeister, Tom de Monse
Architect: Faulkner, Fryer & Vanderpool
Fabricators: American Stone, Inc. (pre-cast stone); Ervite Corp. (porcelain enamel on steel)

Citicorp Barricade

Construction barricades around the sites of new buildings offer some publicity opportunities for the buildings' owners, and also test those owners' sense of responsibility to the surrounding city landscape. Such barricades are prominent in location, being necessarily close to pedestrian eye level, and they remain in such locations for the duration of construction (for a large building, two or three years).

In the heart of Manhattan, the Citicorp organization (formerly First National City Bank) is erecting what promises to be an innovative and attractive building complex—including a 46-floor tower—by the architectural firm of Hugh Stubbins and Associates. Its site is surrounded by a covered pedestrian walkway which is topped with a plywood barricade 12'-high and (except for a minor interruption along a side street) the length of a whole city block's perimeter. Anspach Grossman Portugal, Inc., consultants in marketing communications and design, had previously been commissioned to produce a new public image for the owners, work which resulted in the labels "Citicorp" and "Citibank," and these owners asked the consulting firm to continue its work with a design for the barricade.

The result is bright, snappy, and, considering the great length of the barricade, inventively varied. The most prominent block of the barricade (illustrated here) is

the one facing Lexington Avenue. Because part of the Citicorp Center is to be a new building for St. Peter's Church, the church's corner of the site has its own distinctive look—red and white stripes, as opposed to blue and white stripes in front of Citicorp's own areas. The transition between red and blue is accomplished by stripes of regularly varying width, which also give an appropriate sense of movement down the street. The side street around the corner from St. Peter's will be all red, the other side street all blue, and the Third Avenue section of the barricade will unite the colors with another pattern of stripes.

In addition to this main

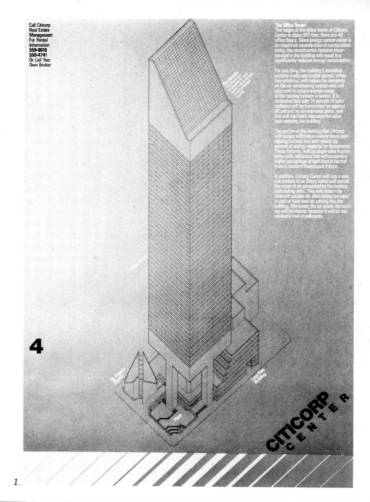

1.

2.

element, posters brighten the pedestrian walk below. These have also been designed by Anspach Grossman Portugal, and show aerial photos of Manhattan, drawings of the new complex, proposed cultural activities (St. Peter's has treated New York for a number of years to jazz concerts, for example), and color photos of striped bass and imported cheeses (much of the complex's retail area will be devoted to an international food bazaar). What might have been dreary is instead quite attractive.

Despite the consideration to the pedestrian that this particular project exudes, the whole Citicorp image-revision program, of which the barricade design is a relatively small part, has some elements

offensive to those of us still stuffy about spelling: will the next generation grow up believing that "city" is spelled "citi," not to mention that "Citibank" is a single word, or that the letter "k" has no body of its own but just one angled stroke following an "n"? Ugh. It's enough to drive one to a "niteklub" for a few "hiballz."

1. Poster shows completed Citicorp tower.
2. Stripes vary as traffic moves along barricade.
3. Other posters suggest activities related to the new complex.
4. View of barricade looking north.

3.

4.

Client: Citicorp Center Management
Design firm: Anspach Grossman Portugal Inc., New York
Designers: Eugene J. Grossman, Daniel Friedman
Architect: Hugh Stubbins and Associates
Fabricator: Walter Sign Co.

University of Petroleum and Minerals, Saudi Arabia

Many of this year's Casebook selections are bilingual, one even multilingual, but none other had to deal with language demands as exotic as those faced by the Interior and Graphics division of Caudill Rowlett Scott (CRS) in its work for the new University of Petroleum and Minerals in Dhahran, Saudi Arabia.

Most obvious of these demands was that the campus graphics had to be not only bilingual but also bi-alphabetical. The school's official academic language is English, but obviously Arabic was needed as well.

Arabic characters are highly calligraphic, derived from a long tradition of hand-lettering and hardly affected by the standardization imposed in other countries by a tradition of moveable lead type. Also, its characters are read from right to left, except for its numerals, which read from left to right (and Arabic numerals, by the way, are quite different in Arabia than they are in Europe and America). Its ascenders and descenders are quite variable in size, and there is not even an *approximate* message length ratio for translations— an Arabic text may be twice the length of its English equivalent, or it may be only half as long. Translations may also vary depending on the region and the translator, and, all in all, the language is not quickly mastered. As one CRS designer put it, "A crash course in Arabic revealed that there are no crash courses in Arabic."

Severe design restraints

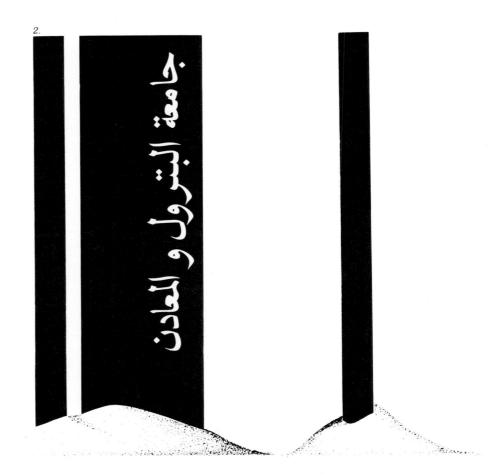

1, 2. Signs in Arabic characters.
3, 4. Grids establish precise letter placement.
5. Campus view.

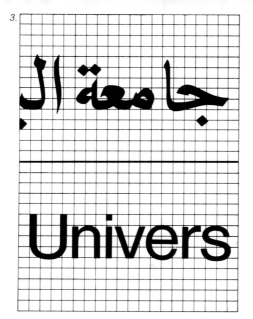

3.

4.

were also imposed by the Saudi Arabian climate: heavy dews with high salt content, 130-degree temperatures, and gale-force winds carrying abrasive sand. Anodized aluminum was chosen as the material best meeting the requirements of both climate and budget. Although salt is a principal enemy of anodic coatings, this disadvantage was offset by aluminum's abrasion resistance, strength-to-weight ratio, and easy availability. A check of existing aluminum signs in similarly salty Galveston, Texas, suggested that good quality anodic coatings could be attractive for a number of years.

The frequently used vinyl letters were avoided in this program because the designers were uncertain of vinyl's reaction to the climate, and because no repair or maintenance crew could be counted on for sign refacing. Instead, for most exterior signs, lettering was color-removed from a field of anodic black; this left the lettering as exposed natural aluminum with some effective reflectivity. As the signs weather, of course, the aluminum will oxidize white, but the designers feel that the loss of reflectivity will be compensated for by the lightening in color. Some silkscreening on matte finish Plexiglas was used in sheltered areas; interior signs were primarily engraved Plexiglas; and some special signs were of molded fiberglass.

Other problems included the fact that most signs had to

5.

be manufactured abroad and shipped to Saudi Arabia. Thus there were considerations not usually crucial: the modularity of the signs, their weight, and all the logistics of shipping, handling, and assembly.

Even the symbols used in this graphics program were curiously limited, in part because there were no familiar precedents in the country, and also because Moslem religious code frowns on pictorial representations, particularly of the human body. (One specific problem, by the way: in a country where men customarily wear robes, those skirts-or-pants silhouettes for rest room symbols must be confusing.)

Despite such a plague of unusual demands, CRS undertook the whole design program for a budget of $22,500, including expenses (not a lot relatively: it's less than one hundredth of one per cent of the total construction budget for this enormous complex). Even more surprising is that all designing and planning for fabrication were accomplished in three months!

Finally, one (perhaps gratuitous) word about a more subtle difficulty overcome by CRS in this work: the difficulty of finding an appropriate style when designing for so unfamiliar a culture. The CRS firm's architects seem to have experienced the problem in designing this university's buildings; although CRS is widely and deservedly admired for its innovations in technology, design and

6.

7.

8.

9.

construction processes, as well as for its handsomely straightforward designs, in this case their buildings look uncharacteristically fussy and ornamented. It is greatly to the credit of the same firm's graphics designers that they have resisted the temptation of such would-be-indigenous styling. The CRS graphics in this case are—like CRS buildings in most other cases—direct, sensible, and appealing.

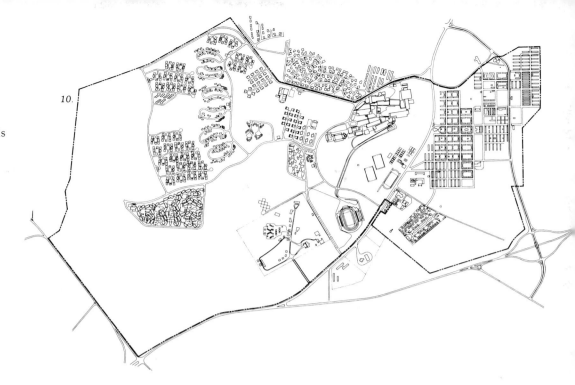

6. Symbol for ladies room (robed men must be careful).
7-9. Bilingual exterior signs have symbols as well.
10. Campus plan.
11. Directory features Arabic on upper line, English translation directly below.
12. Campus silhouette.

مكاتب الادارة
← Administrative Offices ←
مدخل الفريق الزائر
Visitor Team Entrance →
مدخل سيارات الاسعاف →
Emergency Vehicle Entry →

Client: University of Petroleum and Minerals, Dhahran, Saudi Arabia
Design firm: CRS Interior and Graphics, Houston
Designers: Douglas J. Wilson, Jeffry Corbin
Architects: Caudill Rowlett Scott

The 1976 Olympic games in Montreal suffered many difficulties—cheating scandals, political squabbles, and withdrawals—but there were never any reports of people being lost. The shepherding from place to place of such crowds was no small achievement. The signing program devised by Georges Huel & Associates, Inc., included a province-wide network of directional signs, many information signs at the sites of different events, the signs at airports, bus stations, subway stations, railway stations, and on a variety of vehicles.

Remarkable for a program of such scope is the degree of uniformity achieved. This seems partly due to some design restrictions established before Huel's work began—a standard typeface (Univers), a standard "rainbow" of colors, existing pictograms to be repeated, and, of course, a budget. To these, however, the Huel firm added further restrictions. Exterior signs were limited to 18″, 24″, and 34″ vertical sizes, interior signs to 9″, 12″, 18″, and 34″ horizontals. The seven rainbow colors were simplified to five, and, except for the rainbow, color use was limited to specific functions: sports pictograms were all in red, service pictograms were in green, the Univers type and arrows were in white, and all were on a dark blue background.

At the outset of his work (and basic to this whole graphics program), Huel also devised the symbol of the 1976 games, a symbol for

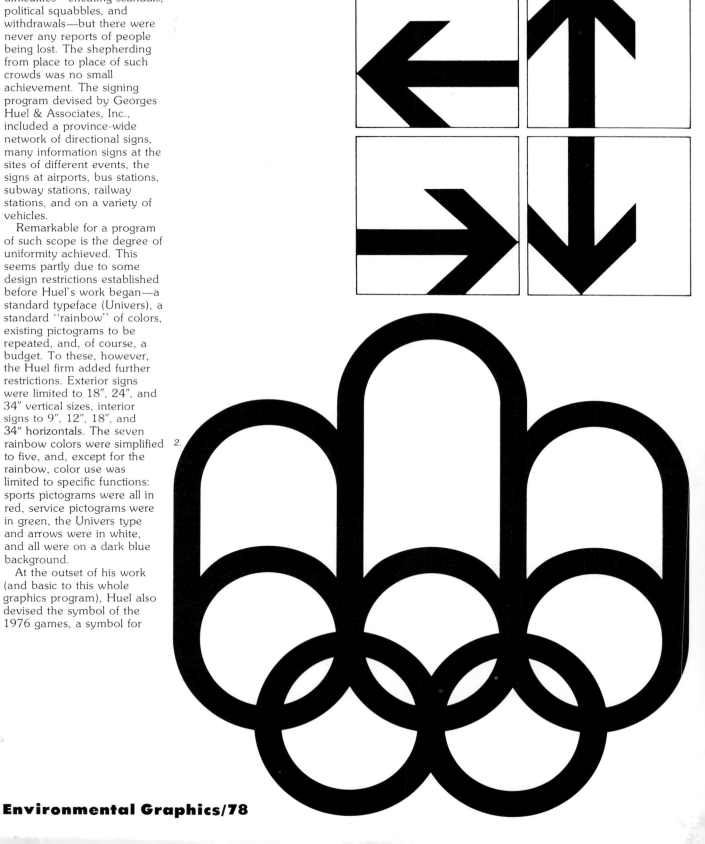

1.

2.

which he also established admirably strict usage controls. Handsome as it is, one may question what it in fact symbolizes: although its five interlocking rings are said to represent international cooperation, the three extended loops at its top are said to suggest the letter "M" (for Montreal), and its central, tallest loop is said to represent the shape of the Olympic track. One wonders how clear all that is to those who don't read the explanation. At the risk of rudeness, may we say that the symbol could just as easily suggest a menacing fist or a hand with its middle finger raised?

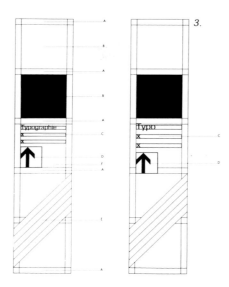

3.

1. Directional arrows, crisp and standardized.
2. The XXI Olympiad symbol, striking, though ambiguous.
3, 4. Lettering sizes and spacings were strictly prescribed.

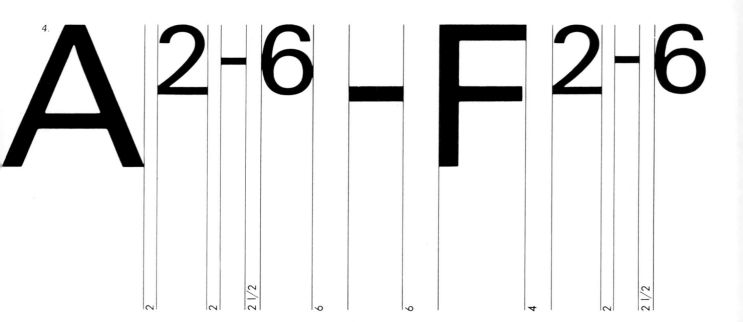

4.

5.

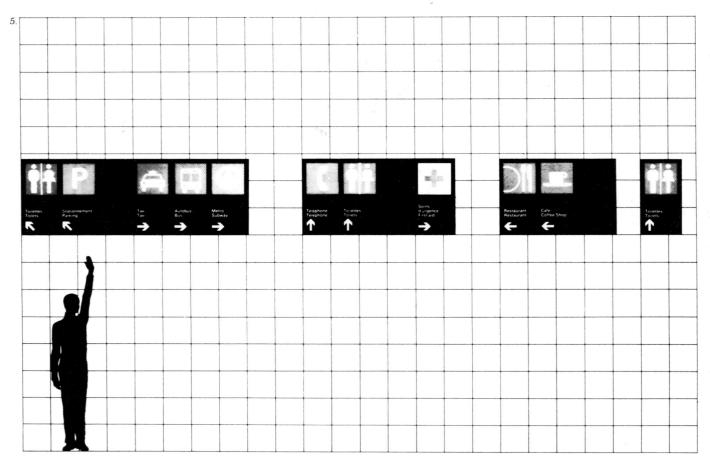

6.

Client: Organizing Committee of the
1976 Olympic Games
Design firm: Georges Huel &
Associates, Inc., Montreal
Consultants: Direction Design;
Consortium Design; Ewart, Tremblay
& Associates
Fabricator: Acme Signalisation

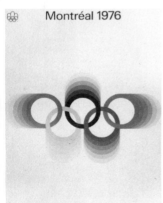

Montréal 1976

Montréal 1976

9.

5. Heights and placement were also specified.
6. Olympic torch-bearer.
7. A. Metro, MUCTC bus, heliport, airport, trains, taxis, buses, women athletes, men athletes. B. Information, lost children, lost and found, bank-exchange, meeting point, tourist office, please remove shoes, sauna, massage. C. Spectators, VIPs, officials, interpreters, tickets, program, hospitality, police, passports.

D. Washrooms, women, men, entrance, exit, stairs, stairs, press, film. E. Smoking, no smoking, silence, no animals, no entry, do not touch, no litter, congress room, computer center. F. Shopping center, souvenirs, newspapers, tobacconist, photo shop, flowers, results room, boat weighing, boat measuring.
8, 9. Two posters from a handsome series, both using the official rainbow colors.

Pontiac Stadium

For a building that is both the world's largest covered stadium and the world's largest air-supported structure, no timid graphics would do. These, designed by the Bloomfield Hills, Michigan, firm of McCoy and McCoy for the Pontiac Stadium (home of the Detroit Lions football team) are appropriately bold, yet with some engaging subtleties.

McCoy and McCoy were hired by the stadium architects (Odell, Hewett, and Luckenbach) and assigned a budget of $100,000 (out of a total architectural budget of $50 million). Although they found this budget rather tight, the designers feel that the imposed constraint had good results for them, precluding any temptations of fussy detailing that would have been inappropriate to the context.

Beginning their work during the building's schematic design phase, McCoy and McCoy were able to participate in basic decisions about movement through the building. Their work concluded with the supervision of sign construction and installation.

With 80,000 football fans to direct to their seats and then, after the game, to the proper exits and back to their cars, a designer's primary goal must be maximum clarity. McCoy and McCoy based their work on considerable research in legibility, and the results are signs of unusual size organized in a system which they call a "binary decision tree" (or, in other words, a progression of simple yes-no decisions for those entering or leaving the stadium).

The first sign encountered in the 200'-wide entrance plaza is a whopping 16' high and 24' long and introduces the color coding of the stadium's three levels. A clever refinement here is that the steel legs supporting this sign are not simply rectangular in configuration, but are 45-degree parallelograms angled to give a non-verbal indication of the entrance direction.

Beyond the plaza, enameled aluminum concourse entrance signs with 6'-high letters are easily visible. Outside ramps take the fans to the proper entrances; then, inside the concourses, 4'-square signs of ¼" aluminum plate direct them to specific seat locations. These last signs are hung from the stadium structure on stainless steel cables fitted with marine hardware. Other concourse information is given on continuous color bands 4' high with letters 2' high.

The bands, and all information pertaining to stadium levels, are coded by color: blue, orange, or green. These colors were chosen not only because they add a festive character to the stadium, but also because they are sufficiently distinct from each other in hue and value, the designers say, to be easily read even by those with an impaired sense of color. Information not pertaining to stadium levels is, appropriately, not in color at all, but in a dark gray.

1. *The inflated stadium structure.*
2-4. *Exterior and interior signs share simple Univers typeface.*
5. *Some exterior signs are expanded to the scale of monumental art.*

2.

3.

4.

5.

Vinyl letters in a Univers typeface have been applied to aluminum and masonry surfaces. The 6′ and 2′ letters have been hand-cut; all smaller sizes are die-cut.

The result of largely utilitarian considerations, the Pontiac graphics program nevertheless achieves a boldness of scale impressively complementary to the power of the stadium's structure and, in addition, contributes some strong color which does much to enliven that structure.

6.

7.

Client: Pontiac Stadium Authority
Design firm: McCoy & McCoy Associates, Bloomfield Hills, MI
Designers: Michael McCoy, Katherine McCoy
Architect: Odell, Hewett & Luckenbach
Fabricator: Colite Industries

6. *Directory outside the stadium.*
7. *Seating information above an entrance to a ring of seats.*

Texasgulf

George Tscherny's environmental graphics program for the Texasgulf Corporation is impressive both in scope—nothing less than worldwide—and in variety—from identifications on company vehicles to identifications on whole buildings. Despite this unusually large range of applications, the program allows an unusually small range of images, thus heightening to the maximum its overall public recognition.

The scope of the program is limited primarily to color and lettering. Color is almost exclusively a pleasant medium blue for a background field, with either black or white lettering; the only exceptions to this rule are the signs with safety, caution, or danger messages, which respectively use green, yellow, or red in accordance with Occupational Safety and Health Act standards.

Lettering is exclusively Helvetica Medium. This is not only because of that typeface's general acceptance and ingratiating character, but also because of its economy in graphics implementations; it is a face readily (and therefore inexpensively) available in stock die-cut vinyl, in cast metal, or in plastic.

Two further details of this graphics program—one highly attractive, one not—deserve notice. Admirable and quite ingenious is the corporation's brief trademark, *Tg*, an attractively unconventional configuration of upper- and lower-case letters which, very appropriately for a company

1, 2. New company signature.
3. Complete company title on glass.

involved in the utilization of
natural resources, recalls the
two-letter identification of
elements on a periodic chart
or in chemistry textbooks.

Less attractive is the
corporation's name, changed
from Texas Gulf, Inc. to
Texasgulf Inc. (without a
comma, please). Corporations
may call themselves whatever
they like, of course, but
non-words like Texasgulf (not
to mention Citibank) do raise
the fear that George Orwell's
''doublespeak'' may be
established long before 1984.

4. *Building sign.*
5. *Symbol on curtain wall.*
6. *Entrance door of a company*
   subsidiary.
7. *Variety of signs in the program.*

4.

5.

Client: Texasgulf Inc.
Design firm: George Tscherny,
Inc., New York
Designer: George Tscherny
Fabricator: Graphic Marking
Systems

Danger–Blasting

Danger
Men Working
Above

Danger
No Smoking,
Matches, or
Open Flames

No Parking

Information →

Texasgulf Canada
Private Property

Tg

Texasgulf Aviation

Tg
← **Tg**
Visitor Parking

Tg
Mine Change House
Main Entrance
Employees Only

Texasgulf
M.L.Weems Lease
R.R.C. No. 05279
500 Acre
Tank Battery

Texasgulf
Private Park
Please call FE 6-3631 for reservations.
Park reserved for
Pick up restroom key at office.
Please help us keep it clean.
No camping in park area.
This park is for your use and enjoyment without charge.

Hamilton Memorial Hospital

One possible approach to the design of graphics for a hospital—and it is an approach difficult to fault—is one of caution. Just as the architecture of the hospital itself can take no liberties at all with, say, the relationship of the operating room to the recovery room, so hospital graphics should take no liberties with clarity just for the sake of style or flair. In a hospital environment as in few others, legibility is a life-and-death matter.

Such an approach was taken by the Atlanta firm of John Muhlhausen Design in its work for the Hamilton Memorial Hospital in Dalton, Georgia. Muhlhausen proves that caution needn't be a bore.

One felicitous addition, bringing character without endangering clarity, is a symbol for the entire hospital operation. Unexpectedly, it is based on Leonardo da Vinci's version of the Vitruvian man. The Roman writer Vitruvius had conceived such a figure (a man with arms extended and feet apart, touching the outlines of both a square and a perfect circle) as proof of the divine order of nature as exemplified by man; the published version of Vitruvius' writings lacked illustrations, however, so it seems to have become a passion of Renaissance theoreticians to attempt to provide a visual reconstruction of Vitruvius' idea, Leonardo's attempt being one of the most famous. Neither Vitruvius nor Leonardo had health care in mind, obviously, much less the Hamilton Memorial

1.A

B

C

Photos: E. Alan McGee

1. A. Special services or outpatient care, bed patient care, concentrated care. B. Maternity care, child care, rehabilitation care. C. Chest x-ray, nurse, shower.
2. "No Entry" sign.
3. Sign at entrance to grounds features, in its upper left corner, an abstraction of the Vitruvian man.

2.

3.

Hospital, yet their symbol—suggesting in this new context a relationship between man's science and man's body—seems ingeniously appropriate.

A further refinement of this restrained graphics program is in the very vocabulary of words it uses. Traditional and pedantic medical nomenclature (such words as podiatry, pediatrics, and obstetrics) has been scuttled in favor of simpler language (foot care, child care, and maternity care). These signs, in many cases, are supplemented with pleasantly designed symbols.

One particular element of the hospital's public spaces—not one in which split-second legibility is likely to be so critical—is given a much more exuberant treatment: an alcove of public telephones is announced by a larger-than-life telephone dial.

Materials used were steel, aluminum, bronze, and formed acrylics. The last material was a substitute on exterior signs for the molded fiberglass of an earlier prototype found to be poorly built and to offer inferior readability when illuminated.

The Muhlhausen office also provided a manual of guidelines for the system's future expansion.

Directory:
Admissions
Child Care
Cafeteria
Emergency
General Care A
Snack Bar
Special Services

Client: Hamilton Memorial Hospital
Design firm: John Muhlhausen Design, Inc., Atlanta
Designer: John P. Muhlhausen
Architect: Abreu & Robeson, Inc.
Fabricators: Colite Industries (exterior signs), Apco Graphics (interior signs)

Special Services

4. Telephone alcove.
5. Typical directory.
6. Sign at department entrance.

Quebec Provincial Parks Signing

The worst thing a parks signing program can do is to be so ostentatious in itself that it detracts from the parks. The signing plan devised by Jacques Guillon/Designers, Inc., for the Department of Tourism of Quebec's Provincial Government has just the opposite character: its components are so understated in size and aggressiveness that they seem to deliver their information in a whisper.

Four feet by eight feet is the size of the largest signs in the system, but many of them are only a modest 6″ square; colors are soft and pleasant, predominantly brown, blue, and white, and materials are intentionally rustic (supporting posts of unpainted wood, for example, rather than the typical steel; even some of the sign faces are of wood).

Within the context of this discreet signing system, an even more discreet detail is the use of miniscule—but still recognizable—*fleurs des lis*. Altogether, the signs, sometimes supplementing French with attractive symbols, have both a discernible flavor of the character of Quebec province and an appropriateness to the serenity of that province's parks.

Despite general admiration for this signing program, however, Casebook jury members detected a lack of rigor in their execution. The signs were obviously meant to have an informal character, yet the designers' resistance to any violation of the environment seems to have allowed the acceptance of

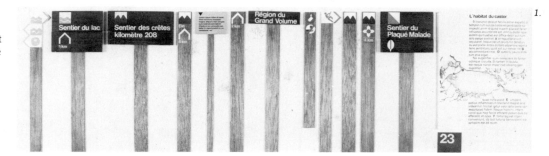

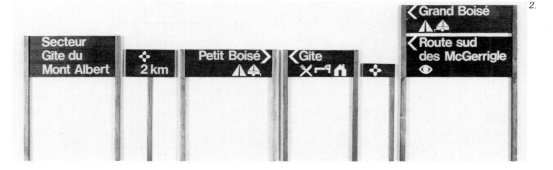

some amateurish construction. This suggests some difficult questions: When does respect for an environment result in signing too meek to convey its directions for getting to that environment? When, if ever, is obviously amateurish craftsmanship preferable to professional work? However difficult it may be to define

such limits, the judges felt that Guillon's self-effacing signs were, on the whole, admirably sensitive to their intended context.

The Guillon firm worked within a design budget of $30,000 and a time limit of one year. Most design decisions and approvals were based on actual full-size mock-ups constructed in

typical park environments. A pleasant aspect of the work, rare indeed in a government commission, was that the designers were responsible directly to a single committee of only three members, all of whom were knowledgeable about the subject and were at a sufficient administrative level to be able to give all necessary approvals.

1-3. Typical signs in the Quebec parks system.

Règlementation   Danger

Identification de lieux (IL)	Identification directionnelle (ID)	Identification de marquage (IM)	Identification de renseignements (IR)	Règlementation d'obligation (RO)	Règlementation d'interdiction (RI)	Règlementation détaillée (RD)	Les messages pictographiques (DA)	Les messages détaillés (DD)

4. Organization chart of sign types, uses, sizes and shapes.

5-8. Examples of the signs in use. Because the signs are constructed of natural wood, they blend well into the parks' environments.

Client: Ministry of Tourism, Province of Quebec
Design firm: Jacques Guillon/Designers Inc., Montreal
Designers: Laurent Marquart, Partner-in-Charge; Morley L. Smith, Jr., Consulting Partner; Luc Courchesne, Project Graphic Designer; Pierre Tardif, Guy Demers, Industrial Designers

93/Environmental Graphics

John Deere
Engine Works

At least since the beginning of the Industrial Revolution, there has been a need for tempering the dehumanizing effects of industrial architecture. It is a need still very much with us, and one which can be answered at least partly by environmental graphics.

The recently built John Deere Engine Works at Waterloo, Iowa, had such a need. It is a straightforward, sensibly ordered building by the Detroit architectural/engineering/planning firm of Smith, Hinchman & Grylls, and it was planned with some thought for the workers. For example, there are employee entrances and cafeterias at both ends of the building to reduce distances between work stations and both parking and lunching areas. But, with almost a million square feet of machinery and production equipment, the place threatened to be pretty dispiriting. Smith, Hinchman & Grylls' own Environmental Graphics group, directed by John Berry, was asked to help in the interior design.

Safety was an obviously important consideration, and the graphics group made certain that such facilities as first-aid rooms, eye-washes, and flooding showers were immediately identifiable and highly visible. Easy-to-read symbols are the primary identification here, with words being supplementary.

Basic also was the need to create identifiable working territories within the building in order to diminish the overwhelming aspect of huge expanses of production floor.

Various machine lines and operation areas were thus given their own particular characters by means of color coding. This not only provides visual variety within the plant; it also, according to Deere's plant engineering manager, Eldon Hansen, encourages better work by heightening each group's sense of identity.

But the fundamental problem at Deere was environmental personality, and the fundamental tool with which the Smith, Hinchman & Grylls group attacked this problem was the use of soft materials. Large overhead signs of sheet metal or other hard, brittle material could have given the desired color as well as all the needed information, but, says designer Berry, they would also have had an unfortunate "guillotine effect," being discomforting to walk under, and they would only have reinforced the plant's industrial atmosphere. What has been designed instead is a system of signs and symbols on vinyl-finished cloth banners which are laced onto frames of inexpensive polyvinyl chloride tubing. Die-cut vinyl letters are glued to the cloth.

While admiring the general effect of these soft graphics, the jury was puzzled by one of the symbols, a hand holding...a needle? a match? what? The hand, in fact, was meant to be holding a coin, seen in profile, and indicating the location of a group of vending machines. "It didn't work," Berry admits, and a redesigned symbol now

1. Engine works exterior.
2-9. The large, potentially impersonal interior has been given considerable personality by signs, symbols and banners—some of them painted on walls in a conventional way—but most of them in a very appealing (and very flexible) "soft" form: cloth laced into suspended frames.

95/Environmental Graphics

shows a hand holding a coin with the coin's face in full view.

But this minor redesign problem points out another advantage of the soft system: its facility for easy and inexpensive change. Compared to the effort of fabricating a new sign of conventional materials, it has been quite easy to stitch up a new banner and lace it into place.

Company recognition of the success of the Waterloo, Iowa, program has led now to the installation of similar graphics in Deere factories in Illinois and Wisconsin.

Client: Deere & Co.
Design firm: Environmental Graphics Group—Smith, Hinchman & Grylls Associates, Inc., Detroit
Designers: John R. Berry, Charles J. Byrne, Marshal Bohlin, Hans Erich Hiedemann, Sonia S. Swigart, William T. Johnston
Architect: Smith, Hinchman & Grylls Associates, Inc.
Fabricator: R.H. Silkscreen

10. Corner detail of a cloth banner laced to a tube frame.
11, 12. Dining areas brightened by murals.
13. The vending machine symbol before its redesign.

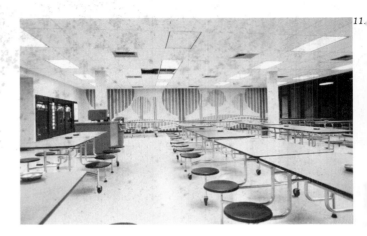

11

12

13

10.